HOLIDAYS

First performed at the West Yorkshire Playhouse on 5th
June, 1995, with the following cast:

Rose	Morag Hood
Arthur	Terence Wilton
Ralph	David Michaels

Directed by John Harrison with Jude Kelly
Designed by Norman Coates
Lighting by Jon Linstrum

The play was also broadcast on Saturday Night Theatre
on 23rd March, 1996, with the following cast:

Rose	Pam Ferris
Arthur	David Horovitch
Ralph	Mark Chatterton

Directed by Michael Fox

Holidays

A play

John Harrison

Samuel French — London
New York - Toronto - Hollywood

CHARACTERS

Rose, late 40s
Arthur, late 40s
Ralph, about 30

The action of the play takes place in a stone cottage in
the Yorkshire Dales in April and a stone cottage in
Provence in June

Production Note

To avoid disturbing the basic reading flow of the text, directions for getting Rose and Arthur into position during scene changes are not always given. The author suggests that directors find their own way of making the transitions. In the original production Arthur was often kept on stage, overlapping briefly and subliminally into the next scene.

ACT I

A stone cottage

Dramatic changes of lighting make it either a cottage in the Yorkshire Dales in April, or a cottage in Provence in June

A ground floor living-room with stone flags gives straight on to the outside and the sky, which is slate-grey for Yorkshire: kingfisher-blue for Provence. Another door to the kitchen. A rickety flight of stairs to a poky loft bedroom. (Alternatively, for those with limited staging facilities, this could be a cubby-hole off the main room)

Yorkshire Lighting up

Rose is sort of unpacking. Marking out her territory. She is in her late forties, but looks a good ten years younger. Bright, compact, attractive, vital but with sudden unexpected drifts into abstraction

Arthur is coming in and out with suitcases, steel saucepans, books. He is of similar age. A lean, thoughtful man, with more cares than he can easily cope with, though he makes a brave show

These activities go on for some time. Finally, Arthur brings a tape recorder

Arthur Where do you want this?
Rose Anywhere for now.
Arthur Sally says you're to talk to it as if she was here.
Rose I know. It's boring she wants me to re-hash it all.
Arthur Something new might come up.
Rose Doubt it.

Pause

Arthur That's it, then.
Rose Will you be all right?
Arthur You know I will.
Rose There's the bean stew for tonight.
Arthur I shall be fine. The supermarkets have practically done away with
the need for marriage. Blessed St Michael.
Rose Some things you can't freeze.

He gives her a loving hug

Arthur Will *you* be all right?
Rose Of course.
Arthur Watch the swallowing.
Rose I shall eat very slowly. Nothing to distract me.
Arthur Because it'll take me hours to get here to thump your back.

Pause

Do you want me to ring at bedtimes? See how you are?
Rose I'll ring you. If I need to. But I'm going to try not to. It's supposed
to be a retreat, isn't it?

They break

I like this place. Reminds me of Mas des Lilas.
Arthur Except the weather.
Rose Don't they have winter in Provence?
Arthur April is supposed to be spring.
Rose Did you see they're lambing in that field at the back?
Arthur I wonder if the telly works.
Rose Sally said it did. I shall only want it for the news.
Arthur You shouldn't be allowed the news on a retreat.
Rose Be a chance to think about it for once. I may not. I shall see.

Arthur pauses at the door. His eyes check round the room

Arthur Steel saucepans. Juicer. Tapes. (*He gestures to the tape recorder*)
Sure you know how to use this?
Rose Yes.

Arthur You don't have to speak into it as if you're reading the news. It'll pick you up almost anywhere in here.
Rose Even shouting from the loo?
Arthur That might perhaps be the dark side of the moon.

Pause

Right. Hate goodbyes.
Rose Haven't had much practice, have we?
Arthur No.

Pause

I love you.
Rose Love you.

They mean this

Drive carefully.
Arthur Of course. Be safe. Till next Saturday then.
Rose Yes.

Arthur goes out

We hear his car start and leave. Rose unpacks an easel and canvas and sets it up for a view out of the window. She switches on and starts to use the tape recorder, while unpacking brushes and paints

Hi, Sally. The cottage is lovely. A dream. Going to be all right here, I know it. Talking to you on this is going to take some getting used to, though. Feels horribly self-conscious. Reminds me of the first one I had when I was a kid. Singing into it. Pretending to be Joni Mitchell. Pretending. That's what I mustn't do, isn't it? You said it ought to feel freer, talking to a machine. I don't think so. I confide in you because you're cosy. Scrumptious. Enveloping. Like eating chocolates on a water-bed. That's what makes you a good counsellor. I do love you, Sally. That's something I can say to the machine without blushing. Couldn't if you were here. So that proves something, I suppose. I'm going to paint the view from this window, I think. And if it's not too bumfreezing I shall do some outdoor stuff down by the beck. We saw a heron fly away as we drove up. I hope he comes back. So I'll start by giving thanks. For so much. For … well, for giving me back belief in myself, I suppose. Don't know where it went. Well… I've never had much self-esteem, have I: you said it. Part of the problem. When they said at the Cancer Centre I'd have to have counselling I didn't know what to expect. Cross betwen confirmation class and those movie clichés of men in horn-rimmed glasses. Certainly not a cross between Madame Arcati and Dawn French. So thanks. And you're wrong to think Arthur resents the time I spend with you. He doesn't. He wants me to do everything I can to get better. You're not his drop exactly: too arty-farty. But he doesn't resent you. His trouble—and my trouble with him, I suppose—is that he's such a relentless unbeliever. And thanks for lending me this cottage. I know it's going to work. I just have a feeling about it. So… You said begin at the beginning. Well … you also said don't be a slave to the clock, so making supper can wait.

She pauses. She switches off the recorder and stares into space

Damn you, Sally. Why do you want me to go over all this old ground? (*She switches it on again*) I just said "Damn you, Sally. Why do you want me to go over all this old ground?" Arthur said perhaps I'd left something out. But I don't think it's that. It's all about facing up to the present, isn't it? All part of arriving at the right conclusion. Bit like the reconstruction Hercule Poirot does in the last chapter before he an-nounces who did it. At the end I'm supposed to come up with the solution, aren't I? The little grey cells against the little grey cells…

She settles in a comfy chair

I suppose it all goes back to Mum's death. That's … fourteen years ago this June. Mum's death. She'd nearly died twice the year before. It was emphysema. As you know. If you remember. She was an unrepentant chain-smoker. Twice I'd sat by her hospital bedside through the night holding her hand. And that wouldn't have been so bad. If she'd let go then. But she clung to life because she was terrified of death. And then when the end did come it was all so sudden and unexpected and I wasn't there … holding her hand. And the afternoon before when I'd visited she'd been in a grump, saying we only wanted to go on holiday to get away from her. Which was true in Arthur's case. And how was she going to manage? But they said at the hospital she was fine. Of course we could go away. The plucky widow had pulled through yet again. What a fighter she was. Ha! I don't think! Struggling up from the bottom of the sea. Sheer panic. That's what it was. Not fight. Not fight as I understand fight. As I have to fight now. Every day. Every hour. And it was all so unseemly. She died all alone and hating us. Me. Us. When we rang in the morning... "We're so sorry, Mrs Plumridge passed away peacefully in the night." Passed away peacefully be buggered. Dragged down screaming more like. So unseemly. So rushed. We'd had the damned holiday booked for yonks, you see. And everyone advised us to go. We'd been every year for the past ... oh, I don't know ... three, four. Arthur was needing it. Looking forward to it. The job really knackers him. All that hanging on the money markets. All that sweating over green screens. All that shouting. He's getting too old for it. He always says he could never cope without the month in France. The cottage was beginning to feel like ours. Mas des Lilas. We still have it for the whole of June every year. I love the morning light in Provence. And the deep nights with the stars.

The Lighting begins to change

But there was something gross about piling on the ferry just two days after the funeral. And in Mum's car to boot, because our own was in dock for some reason... Forget now. We'd said my sister and brother-in-law could inherit her car, but they said you borrow it first for your holiday. Because ours was in dock. I tried. I really tried. In the photos I look quite happy. Grinning up out of the pool. Pool of tears.

Lighting changes to Provence. It is a star-filled night

Rose is awake and crying softly

Arthur raises himself on his elbow

Arthur Rose...? Are you crying, Rose?
Rose (*through tears*) What do you think?
Arthur Come here. (*He comforts her*) What are you crying for? Mum still?

Rose Mum still! Just because you're glad she's dead——
Arthur Don't be ridiculous.
Rose Don't try to deny it. That's no help.
Arthur I'm relieved, I suppose. She didn't exactly make life easy for us. You cried on the boat out. You cried most of the drive down. How long's it going to go on?
Rose It's only been two weeks, you bastard. Got to have a bit of grief.
Arthur She was a selfish old bitch and a drunk.
Rose I know she was. That's not the point. She was still my mother and I should have been there. I can't forgive myself for that.
Arthur But the hospital thought she was OK.
Rose Yes, all right. Just let me cry.
Arthur Not much of a holiday.
Rose No. Well. We shouldn't have come.
Arthur I thought you were really enjoying yourself on the beach yesterday.
Rose I was. Go back to sleep.
Arthur Can't sleep with you weeping.
Rose Well, go for a walk or something.
Arthur I'm tired.
Rose Well, go downstairs then. Sleep on the sofa.
Arthur Thanks a bomb. I wouldn't sleep, knowing you were up here crying.
Rose Well, comfort me then.
Arthur I am.
Rose Like a pee-soaked blanket.
Arthur Thanks.
Rose You're welcome.

They turn away from each other

Arthur Rose...?
Rose Mmm...?
Arthur You must admit it hasn't been all beer and skittles.
Rose I've never denied it. She was jealous of you.

Pause

And you of her.

Arthur I bloody wasn't.

Rose Bloody was. Jealous of the time I had to spend with her.

Arthur That's not the same. I just couldn't cope with the bloody drinking.

Rose Neither could I.

Arthur She wouldn't have done it if she'd really loved you.

Rose Oh... (*Meaning "Don't be ridiculous"*) She was sick.

Arthur And a rotten mother. She was already drinking you to death when you were in the womb.

Rose (*angrily*) There's nothing wrong with me.

Arthur Not yet.

Rose (*getting out of bed*) Christ, I can't listen to this. God, you are an insensitive pig sometimes. (*She comes downstairs to sink crying into an armchair*)

After a while, Arthur heaves himself out of bed and follows her. He stands looking at her uncertainly from the foot of the stairs

Arthur Sorry. I'm so tired I don't know what I'm saying.

Pause

I just can't get on the wavelength. I can't mourn her. (*He comes closer*) We did everything we could. Everything it was our duty to do. More than either of your sisters did.

Rose She relied on me.

Arthur She knew you were the soft touch. The others are too like her. Hard bitches.

Rose So that's my family written off. You really know what to say to help, don't you?

Arthur Oh, come on. You were always the cuckoo in the nest.

Pause

Sweet cuckoo.

Pause

Married to an insensitive pig.

Pause

Onk. Onk.

Pause

Let's go for a stroll in the moonlight. Please. I can apologise better out there.

Pause

Rose You do have good ideas sometimes. I'll get my sandals...

Arthur wanders on to the patio to wait for her and ambles slowly out of sight

Yorkshire Lighting up

What you don't realize, Sal, is that it's been in some ways worse for Arthur. You see, he was told things I wasn't. Apparently, when the secondaries appeared, about three months after the mastectomy, Dr Frankenstein looked at him sadly and said there wasn't much hope because of my age. Not a case of Too Young to Die but Too Young to Live. Because of the bloody disease being hormone dependent. If I'd passed the change I'd have been a better life. As I believe they say in the insurance trade. Of course, I didn't know any of this. I was all fight and hope and trust in the clever doctors. My grandpa'd been a doctor so I'd been brought up to venerate them. And Arthur kept that black fear to himself for seven whole years ... until the bugger came sneaking back in my lungs and then even *I* was told I'd be lucky to see the summer. Arthur just said "we've been here before, Rosie, don't listen to them." And that's when he told me I'd already defied their gloomy bloody prognostications for seven whole years. Fantastic. And that's when we decided to spit in the eye of the medics and go to the Cancer Help Centre. Seven years ago. Lucky number, seven, isn't it? Has been for me. On the whole. Started the diet and the meditation and the visualisation and all the rest of it. Discovered there were actually things I could do to help myself. I didn't have to just lie there like a monkey on a slab. Somehow the medics can't help infecting you with their own helplessness and despair. Even the nicer ones. In fact the nicer they are, the more despairing they tend to get. Not old Frankenstein. One day we dared to ask him what he thought the chances were. "Forty—sixty," he said breezily. We didn't dare ask him in whose favour. But the Centre—and particularly you, dearest Sally—gave me the best medicine—hope. But I'm wasting tape, aren't I? I started out to put in a plug for Arthur because I feel you mistrust him. Don't. I can handle my doubts there. I know he's selfish. Aren't all men? I also know he loves me.

Provence Lighting up

They are packing up from that same holiday

Arthur It's been good, Rose, hasn't it?
Rose Uh-uh.
Arthur It's difficult to keep all the good bits together when we're home and I'm working.
Rose Maybe you don't have to work so hard.
Arthur Take your eye off the ball for a second and you're out of the game. And it pays for all this.
Rose But if we're just living for one month out of twelve...
Arthur It's not that bad, surely?
Rose I never said it was. It was you who said it was difficult to cling on to the good bits.
Arthur Yes. I just meant I was going to make a special effort.
Rose At least you won't have Mum to cope with.
Arthur I did try. Sometimes.
Rose Sometimes. Not very often.
Arthur Neither did she.
Rose That's true.
Arthur There'll be her flat to get rid of.
Rose I can deal with that. Sorting out all her stuff's going to be a nightmare.
Arthur Hope it won't be too depressing. Don't want you round there surrounded by damp hankies.
Rose Got to cry somewhere. You don't like me doing it around you.
Arthur Because I don't like to think you're unhappy.
Rose I don't think grief is about being unhappy, quite. It's a reflex. Like shedding a skin or something. Have you seen my travel iron?
Arthur Yes, it's in the kitchen. I used it on my shorts.
Rose Ridiculous to iron shorts you're going to be driving in. Did you do mine?

Arthur No. As you say, it would have been ridiculous.

Rose (*on her way to the kitchen for the iron*) Taking the Alps route or the Rhône?

Arthur You'd rather the Alps, wouldn't you?

Rose I'd love it. Thought you might be worried about time.

Arthur It's boring pounding up the autoroute. We might try for a couple of nights at St. Firmin.

Rose I thought you'd be in a hurry to get back.

Arthur I'm never in a hurry to get back. It just sucks me in when I'm there. But I'm really going to try this time. I'm full of good resolutions.

Rose So am I. I think. Wish it wasn't her car though.

Yorkshire Lighting up. Dense smoke billows from the kitchen

Rose backs out spluttering

Oh Christ Almighty, what's the matter with the buggering thing? (*She staggers to the phone and picks up a hand-written list*) Plumber? Electrician? Oh, thank God. Aga. (*She dials a number*) Can I speak to Mr Grayling, please? … Oh, well, you don't know me, my name's Rawsthorne and I'm staying in Miss Goodwin's cottage at … yes, that's right. And I'm having terrible trouble with the Aga. And your name's on the list as… Smoking. Belching smoke.… Yes, I've tried that.… No, I don't think so. Well, it's pretty chronic actually. … Could you? Tonight? … That's awfully kind. I'm alone here and desperate. … What? (*She laughs*) No, not the sort of thing one should say on the telephone, I quite agree. Right. Half an hour? That's wonderful. Thanks. (*She puts the phone down*) Sounds a larky gent.

She gives a big relieved sigh and switches on the tape recorder

Sally, my cover is about to be blown. I mean, I'm being forced out of retreat. Well, it's this bloody witches' cauldron of yours. I don't know how you cope with it. Yes, I know they're a status symbol. I've rung your Mr Grayling. Sounds a good old country name. Anyway, where was I? Half an hour to kill. Let me get a refill.

She pours herself a glass of white wine

Thank God the diet allows wine. I'd have gone bonkers. Two glasses of *good* wine what's more. It was a happy goodbye to plonk when I started on the diet. Seven years. God. Mind you, I don't miss meat at all. Or dairy products really. I always said I'd never be able to give up cheese but it's amazing what you can give up if you're convinced your life depends on it. I rather like life. As you know. So where was I?

She settles down

I said it went back fourteen years to Mum's death. But I suppose it really goes further. If we're talking about things that troubled me inside. Goes back to when we couldn't agree about having a child. I wanted one. Arthur didn't. I accused him of marrying me under false pretences. He wavered a bit. We postponed. And postponed and postponed. And then this happened. I mustn't blame it all on Arthur though. I could have left the cap out, couldn't I? That's what my best friend Liz advised. Leave the bloody cap out. He'll never know. But I couldn't cheat on him. I love him. I really do. He's not the villain of the piece. In fact, he held me together when I'd had me tit off. He wrote this lovely poem about the scar ... how we must love it ... the scar ... as if it were an eyebrow or a belly button...

"...the scar is you.

the scar is you healing..."

I mean, not many financial wizards write poetry in their spare time, do they? Well, I've never done a head count. T. S. Eliot. He worked in a bank. And Trollope was in the Post Office, wasn't he? Not that he was a poet. I'm rambling. Still, I suppose that's good. Means I'm getting more relaxed with this thing. Which will probably reward me by running out of tape. There I go. Negative thinking again. Shit... Anyway, there we were, at Mas des Lilas. Six months after the op. I was raw in every pore.

Provence Lighting up. Mid-morning sunshine

Arthur comes in from outside shaking a bathing towel

Arthur Come on, Rosie. Today we're going for our first swim.
Rose Wonder if I dare.
Arthur Why else did we buy that expensive bathing costume?
Rose I haven't tried it on since Madame Thing's.

Arthur So try it on now.

Rose What if the bloody prosthesis pops out? On a crowded beach?

Arthur It won't. Honestly, in the shop I couldn't see the join.

Rose That was Madame's poking and prodding.

Arthur Well, I'll poke and prod. And not only there.

Rose Arthur...

A moment of silence

Thank you for loving me.

Arthur It's a pleasure.

Rose I mean ... thank you for still ... being able to make love to me.

Arthur Lucky man. Got me an Amazon.

Rose Why?

Arthur The Amazons used to slice off one tit to show what superwomen they were.

Rose Christ!

Arthur Not many of them about.

Rose Did you ... did you think it was going to be difficult? I mean they always say men are either bum people or tits people and you've always been both.

Arthur No, I'm definitely a bum and one tit person. Rose. It's about loving you. Not bums or tits. I mean, I love them because they're your bum and tit.

Rose Supposing they have to take the other?

Arthur Then you'll be a hermaphrodite. Equally special. Anyway, they won't. They've got it all out now. They said. All the nasties.

Rose Still got to have the three-monthly check-up.

Arthur That's just routine. Come on. We're wasting sunshine—get into that sexy costume.

Arthur bustles out to get his espadrilles from the patio

Yorkshire Lighting up

Rose still confides to the machine

Rose He was wonderful. He led me through that time by the hand as if I were his child. It could have been awful. I could feel it so for him. The mutilation. They'd been cutting his woman about. But he was all positive. Upbeat. Encouraging me back to work: carrying on as if nothing had happened. (*She pauses*) I wonder... I can almost hear you, Sally. You're saying "but something had happened." Were we just denying it? Pretending it hadn't? Pretending? There may be something there I've got to look into. I only know it felt wonderful at the time. And he was holding my hand at all these quarterly check-ups. We lived through the suspense together. Until finally Dr Frankenstein said he thought we could make them half-yearly ... that was a celebration night and a half ... or it should have been. I must tell you, the night before I went in for the original mastectomy we'd been to see *Annie Hall* and we laughed like drains. So when we noticed—co-incidence, co-incidence— it was on again at the local flea-pit we simply had to go and, do you know, we didn't laugh once? We must have been in some sort of shock. We'd forgotten how to handle good news. Tragedy had been easier. Well, you go into overdrive, don't you?

A knock at the door

Hang on, there's your chap. (*She switches off the tape recorder and answers the door*)

Ralph Grayling is there. He is about thirty. Light Yorkshire accent, but no hayseed. Chunky, physical, though an enquiring mind peers out

Ralph Mrs Rawsthorne? Aga trouble?
Rose Oh, wonderful. Come on in.
Ralph Been smoking, has it?
Rose The understatement of the century.
Ralph Someone should give it a government health warning.
Rose Mr Grayling, is it?
Ralph Yes, here's my ID. (*He hands her a business card*) Never let anyone in without an ID nowadays. Could be Jack the Ripper.

Rose raises her eyes challengingly from the card and hands it back

That wasn't funny, was it? Sorry. Very sorry.

Pause

I'll go straight to it, then, shall I? The beast knows me of old. I don't
think he'll bite.

Rose I can't even offer you a cup of coffee.

Ralph That's all right. I've had me tea.

*He goes into the kitchen and we hear him clonking about. Rose watches
from the door*

Rose I've never used one of these things before.

Ralph (*off*) They're all right once you've got the hang. On holiday, are
you?

Rose Yes.

Ralph (*off*) On your own?

Rose I'm tempted to say don't be nosey.

Ralph (*off*) Quite right. Never could mind me own business. You'll be
cosy here once we've got this going.

Even more smoke billows out

(*Off*) Got to get worse before it gets better.

Rose God, how true they are, these old wives' sayings. Like what Noël
Coward said about popular songs.

Ralph (*off*) What did he?

Rose "So potent. Cheap music."

Ralph (*off*) Is that right? Talked like that, did he?

Rose That's the imitation everyone does. He was before my time.

Ralph (*off*) Mind if I turn the radio on? I like a bit of cheap music while
I work.

Rose It's tuned to Radio Three.

Ralph (*off*) Soon change that. You mind?

Rose No. Of course. Let's have a rave-up.

Ralph (*off*) What?

Rose I said if it helps to get the work done...

*Ralph turns the kitchen portable on out of sight and twiddles to Radio One.
Rose comes back to the tape recorder and switches it on*

(Sotto voce, *to the machine*) I'm getting silly. Only been alone five
minutes and I'm chirping like a grass widow. Your Mr Grayling...

Where did you find him? I believe you're an even darker horse than I imagined. Anyway ... while he consoles himself with Radio One and I wait for a sign from blessed Aga... I'll go back to Provence. So many holidays. So many times when we even forgot I had cancer.

Provence Lighting up. Hot

Arthur is reading in the shade of the doorway

Rose is clearing the lunch away

If we'd had one when we were first married it'd be thirteen now.

Arthur That's a complicated way of saying we've been married thirteen years.

Rose No, I mean those baby years are so short. So soon over. We'd have had a teenager by now——

Arthur Into heavy metal and drugs.

Rose They aren't all.

Arthur You mean ours would have been sharing Radio Three and Chekhov with us?

Rose Don't see why not.

Arthur And preferring gourmet French food to fish and chips?

Rose Don't see why not. The French kids all do. I think it's wonderful the way even little tiddlers sit there solemnly through a five course midi.

Arthur Won't last. The McDonalds are spreading, tra-la, tra-la...

Rose I think that's sad.

Arthur So do I.

Pause

Rose There'd have been three of us.

Arthur Why not four or five?

Rose Why not?

Arthur You're determined to be broody today.

Rose It isn't a thing you determine. It just happens.

Pause

Anyway, it's all water under the bridge now, isn't it?

Arthur I suppose so.

Rose You can still conceive if you have cancer. The baby doesn't have
    to be affected.
Arthur Wouldn't like to chance it.
Rose Not good stock? You think like a bloody farmer.
Arthur Wouldn't like to risk it for you, I meant. Your body's got quite
    enough to cope with.
Rose Not just my body.
Arthur (*putting his book down*) Are you determined to have a row?
Rose I wouldn't mind.
Arthur It's too hot.
Rose Let it all out in thunder and lightning. Then have a sleep.
Arthur There are better things we could do. And then have a sleep.
Rose Not in the mood. Unless...
Arthur What?
Rose Unless I can leave the cap out.
Arthur Don't be bloody frivolous.
Rose May be frivolous to you. Isn't to me.
Arthur Rose. You're not making sense.
Rose Is it important to make sense?
Arthur It's important to think things through.
Rose Feelings are important too.
Arthur Well of course they are.
Rose And they don't go away as easily as thoughts.
Arthur I love you.
Rose Um...
Arthur Isn't that enough any more?

Pause

Rose Not always.

Arthur, disturbed, picks up his book and exits

Yorkshire Lighting up

*Rose is unpacking some of her canvases and standing them around. She
unhooks a calendar and hangs an abstract in its place on the wall*

*Ralph comes out of the kitchen, dusting off his hands on his handker-
chief*

Ralph There you go. Shouldn't have any more trouble now.
Rose Thanks very much. How much do I owe you?
Ralph Oh, I'll send Miss Goodwin a bill. It's her Aga.
Rose It was good of you to come out so quickly.
Ralph Think nothing of it. (*He nods at the abstract*) I like that.
Rose Thanks.
Ralph Why? Did you do it?
Rose Yes.
Ralph You a proper painter or is it just a hobby?
Rose Good question. I was trained as a proper painter.
Ralph What's it supposed to be?
Rose My thoughts.

Pause

Ralph I suppose it's easier to live with them if you put them on canvas.
Rose That's...
Ralph Bright for an odd-job man?
Rose No, I...
Ralph 'S all right. You do any job you can get nowadays. Your average
meter reader's an honours graduate.
Rose Did you...?
Ralph General Science at Manchester. It was meant to turn out new
Renaissance Man. Actually I went into mine management. Made
redundant six years ago. Went round the world on me redundancy pay
so now I do whatever's going. I'll be off, then. (*He moves to the door,
glancing briefly at the other paintings as he goes*) Well, have a good
holiday——
Rose Thanks.
Ralph Get any more trouble, you know where to find us. Actually, I might
look back in a day or two. See if that flue's still drawing——
Rose There's no need. I mean, I can always ring you. Anyway, I should
probably be out. I intend to do a lot of walking.
Ralph Great walking country. You must go up Drybank Fell. Got me own
key, actually. Miss G. likes me to look in from time to time. Would that
bother you? If you weren't here?
Rose I suppose not.
Ralph You can ask her about me.
Rose No, that's all right. But I'm supposed to be on a sort of retreat. You
know, on my own. No visitors.

Ralph I didn't think you meant *Retreat from Moscow*.

Rose Sorry. I don't mean to be condescending.

Ralph 'S all right. So it would actually be best if I came when you were out, wouldn't it?

Rose If it's really necessary, I suppose so.

Ralph Well, it's quite an old Aga. Needs coddling. Wouldn't want you to be smoked out again. I'd only go in the kitchen. You could even leave the washing-up, if you like.

Rose (*laughing*) I might do that.

Ralph Not promising. Good. Well—I won't see you then. Bye.

Rose Goodbye. Drive carefully.

Ralph is gone

Why the fuck did I say that?

Long ago in Provence

Their first holiday at Mas des Lilas

Unpacking. Arthur setting things out downstairs

(*Calling from upstairs*) Have you *seen* the painting in the bathroom?

Arthur (*laughing*) Yes.

Rose (*off*) Way out!

Arthur I think it must be a throw out from one of his early exhibitions.

Rose appears

Rose God, aren't we lucky?

Arthur (*agreeing*) Lucky.

Rose It actually being a painter's cottage. With all his bits and pieces. Not some faceless holiday gîte. Do you think we could come here every year?

Arthur Don't see why not. As long as I continue to make sufficient dosh.

Rose I might even get inspired. Get working again.

Arthur You don't need to.

Rose What do you mean?

Arthur Well, I mean, of course you can paint. What I mean is you don't have to think of it as work. Exhibitions and that. You're not starving in a garret. You've got me now to provide.

Rose Arthur, I never starved in a garret. I was doing rather well. I only stopped because... I don't know why I stopped.

Arthur It doesn't matter.

Rose Oh, but it does. I think I stopped because ... well, we were new, and there was setting up home, playing house... You're not jealous of my working, are you, Arthur?

Arthur Of course not. Didn't I encourage you to get that job in the gallery?

Rose Part time. Selling other people's paintings. That's not the same. In fact, that's probably another reason why I've dried up. But here I feel ... the light and everything...

Arthur Certainly worked for Cézanne.

Rose Yes. Pity that's all been done. No point turning out plagiarisms for tourists. But I might find my own reaction to it all. In time.

Pause

Arthur Rose...
Rose What?
Arthur You won't paint all the time though, will you?

She looks at him, puzzled

I might get lonely.

Yorkshire Lighting up slowly to wind and weather

Rose comes in swathed in outer garments which she begins to peel and shake, wind-blown and wet, stamping her feet warm. As soon as she can make it, she turns on the tape recorder. She needs to share

Rose Gosh, Sally, what a day! I had to share my last nut bar with a gang of angry geese or I wouldn't be here now. Nothing else would appease them. Phew! I need a drink. First of the two glasses. (*She pours*) Are you counting? (*She drinks*) Ah, that's better. Do you know I was up before seven this morning? Yes, me! Went up and meditated by the waterfall. Shone light in all my dark places. Talking of which, last night the stars

were incredible. I stood on the back lawn and God lit up the whole bang
shoot for me. I could see both the big plough and the little plough and
all those others I'm always going to learn but never do. It was almost as
good as Provence, apart from freezing your knackers off. Girls don't
have knackers, do they? But it's a nice ugly word. So back to this
morning. I did Tai Chi in the meadow among the sheep. Then I came
home and had a huge bowl of porridge sitting in the porch wrapped to
the nines. Home. Did you notice how easily that slipped out? Blessed
Aga is behaving so far. I don't know whether Grayling's wandering in
and out. He's certainly left no spoor. And he certainly hasn't done my
washing up. So then I decided on the big walk. Packed my rucksack with
apples and nut bars and the map and set off for Linton. Oh, and the
binoculars. Mustn't forget them. They've been heaven. I've watched all
the birdies. Yellow, grey and pied wagtails. Wrens up really close. And
a dipper making its nest. No heron today though. And lambs, newly born
and all bloody still. Being a tiny part of such fertility seems the most
healing thing. The dark side is always there too, though. Found a dead
baby rabbit. Grey, grey under the sky and so sweet. Gave it a burial
service. Said that bit from *The White Devil* that Arthur likes so much…
"Call for the robin red breast and the wren…" Do you know it?

> "Call for the robin red breast and the wren,
> Since o'er shady groves they hover,
> And with leaves and flow'rs do cover
> The friendless bodies of unburied men.
> Call unto his funeral dole
> The ant, the field-mouse and the mole,
> To rear him hillocks, that shall keep him warm.
> But keep the wolf far thence…"

—and said a prayer and teed it under the earth. Thought of mortality,
what else? I'm not afraid of it, Sally. Thanks to you. But I'm not ready
for it yet either. I'm too young, for Christ's sake. Could make good use
of at least another twenty years. And I don't want to leave Arthur behind.
We go everywhere together.

Where was I? Oh, yes, it's been communal eating day. I had to share my
lunch with some greedy ducks sheltering beneath a wall, because the
weather suddenly got dramatic. He really put on a show for me.
Thunder. Lightning. Snow. Threw in the lot. But he couldn't frighten
me. I ran into the middle of the field and did Tai Chi in a blizzard.
Thrilling. Evoke blue skies and here they are. Wonderful. Mind over

matter. Another of those silly little phrases we take for granted. (*She pauses*) Birds are so ... exclusive, aren't they...? Flap their wings and leave the rest of us behind ... flight... We always bird-watch in Provence. And butterfly-watch. Another kind of flight... So fragile. Like hope... God, there's posey for you. We don't do it very seriously. Just for fun.

Provence Lighting up

Rose and Arthur are poring over butterfly books

Arthur I think it was a Bright-eyed Ringlet.

Rose Let me see. No, look, it didn't have these white centres to the eye-spots.

Arthur Could it have been a Dewy Ringlet?

Rose What makes you think so?

Arthur I don't know. I just like the name. These books are always bloody useless every year. The colour printing's all wrong.

Rose Fun though.

Arthur I find them exasperating. I think we should invent our own names. What we saw was a Tipsy Two-tailed Rawsthorne's Cracker.

Rose If you say so.

Arthur You know, Rose, I hardly noticed any of these things before I met you.

Rose And you a poet.

Arthur Oh, that was all about me growing up. Until I met you, I had no time for insects.

Rose But you always walked in the country. It was you who taught me.

Arthur Yes, plodding along with my nose in the air. They were thinking walks, not noticing walks. I could have been anywhere from Gravesend to Burma.

Rose Still, if you hadn't made me walk, I shouldn't have taken up noticing. Never noticed much when I was a kid apart from what was in the pop charts.

Arthur How nice we've both got things to thank each other for. Perhaps we should do that more regularly. You know, like a sort of secular grace. *Grace à Deux*. I thank you, oh Rosie, for introducing me to insects, to all the birds and beasties of the field, even things that crawl.

Pause

Your turn.

Rose Oh. I thank you, Arthur, for introducing me to music. And books I'd never have opened. And poems galore.

Arthur I thank you, Rosie, for improving my taste in food.

Rose Before the diet of course.

Arthur I don't know. You do pretty well even with that.

Rose But you can't thank me for getting cancer and worrying us both silly.

Arthur Don't you think it's brought us closer?

Rose Yes. Perhaps it has.

Arthur You said we had to learn to love it. Respect it. Not let it see us always as angry defenders. And then perhaps it'd go away.

Rose Yes. Sally said it, actually.

Arthur Whoever. So I can thank it too. Through you. Are you there, ancient beast? We love you. There. In the name of the Rose and the Rose and the Rose. For ever and ever. Amen.

Rose It's a nice idea. You do have good ideas, Arthur.

Yorkshire Lighting up

And he does, Sally. Smashing ideas. And he's been faithful. We both have. Not bad, eh? Well, you probably think we're chicken. Not opening ourselves to experience or something. But if you've got everything you could reasonably want, why bugger it up? Oh, I can hear you, you monster. You're saying "but you haven't got everything you want". That's making use of privileged information! But who has, Sally? Tell me that. Have you? No, that's not fair. You haven't come to me for counselling. I can imagine your spectacles slipping down your nose in disgust. "Am I singing my own song", you're asking, aren't you, in the immortal words of Dr Le Shan. I'm a bit disturbed today. I seem to have lost all the lovely joy of yesterday. First of all, today's walk wasn't as successful as yesterday's. Just too fucking cold. I was a bit gutless about it. I got to the top of the Fell all right, which was great, and let myself be blown about for a while—blowing all the cancer to buggery, I hoped. But then I came over all listless and just hurried down. And then—when I came in—I wasn't alone.

Rose is coming in from her daily walk

Ralph emerges from the kitchen

Ralph Sorry. I was just going.

Rose Everything all right?

Ralph Yes. Working a treat. Been far?

Rose Took your advice. Went up Drybank Fell.

Ralph Good for you.

Rose Would you like a cup of tea?

Ralph Thought you were on retreat.

Rose I've been retreating all day. Won't hurt me to have a bit of company for tea.

Ralph Actually, kettle's singing.

Rose You've made yourself one?

Ralph Oh, no. Lord, no. Just filled it to test the hot plate.

Rose Right. Actually... I've just realized. I haven't got any ordinary tea. And no milk. I drink herb teas.

Ralph Miss Goodwin keeps her tea bags in the cupboard over the sink. And I can drink it without milk.

Rose Oh, good. (*She prepares tea*) The view from the top was sensational.

Ralph Pity it's too far to carry your easel.

Rose Oh, I could probably do it from memory. Actually, I wouldn't want to paint just what it looks like. I'd want to paint the experience of being up there.

Ralph I'd be happy if I could paint what it looks like.

Rose You can do that with a camera. Do you paint at all?

Ralph Me? No. Lord, no.

Rose Well, the most unexpected people do. I don't mean you'd be unexpected, not at all. That's why I asked.

Ralph I meant to be gone before you got back. Thought maybe you'd stay out while dark.

Rose Looked like more snow, so I hurried. I got soaked through yesterday and I didn't fancy drying out another lot of clothes.

Ralph Don't want to be getting a chill with the weather this chancy.

Rose Oh, no, I'm very sensible. I got straight into a lovely deep bath and my clothes steamed over the Aga. It was all very primitive and satisfying.

Ralph I grew up in a place like this. But even more primitive. No Aga. No bathroom. Just a tin tub in front of the fire on Saturday nights.

Rose I thought that sort of life went out fifty years ago.

Ralph Not up in these Dales. Mind you, I've got Mum and Dad sorted out now in a nice new bungalow with all mod cons. Most of these places were going derelict until the posh folks started doing them up for holidays.

Rose Posh folks like Miss Goodwin and me?

Ralph If you like.

Rose I'm not posh, Mr Grayling. Don't let the accent fool you.

Ralph I'm always a bit wary of southerners.

Rose You who've been round the world! Where actually did you go?

Ralph Yugoslavia first. Before all the fighting. I had a mate there worked in the travel business. Greece. Bummed round the Greek islands until I'd had enough salad. Then got on a ship to Bombay. Up to Delhi. Saw the Taj Mahal and the beggars. Couldn't stand the beggars so I got another boat to Australia. Worked my way across from Perth to Sydney. Too much sunshine. You miss the grey skies. Cross the Pacific to SF— San Francisco. Just as pretty as it looks in the movies. Cross the States by Greyhound bus. Several months in Chicago. Had a bad experience in New York. Flew home before the money ran out.

Rose Gosh. How ordinary you make it all sound.

Ralph You travelled much?

Rose Not round the world. Not to far-off places. Italy. Austria. Portugal. Mostly the holiday spots. We go to France every summer.

Ralph I've never been there.

Rose Good heavens. You go round the world and miss out France.

Ralph It seemed too near like to bother. I didn't go to the Isle of Man either.

Rose I'm tempted to say there's no comparison. So what did it do for you? Going round the world?

Ralph Do for me? Well. Proved Columbus was right, I suppose. You *can* start out in one direction and come back from the other.

Rose Must have done more than that.

Ralph Got me a suntan.

Rose In other words, you're not saying.

Ralph What sort of thing do you want me to say?

Rose Well … crossing the States by bus, for instance. That must be an amazing experience. The sheer size of it.

Ralph Mostly mile after mile of nothing punctuated by gas stations. Makes mankind seem very impermanent.

Rose That's the sort of thing I mean. Did you go alone?

Ralph To start with. Met plenty of folk along the way.

Rose How brave. I've never been anywhere on my own. That's why I'm here this week.

Ralph And I'm spoiling it.

Rose Oh … no. No—you're one of the folk I'm meeting on the way.

Ralph I reckon you need never be alone. If you choose. And yet you're always alone. Really.

Rose That's rather profound.

Ralph Ah, well.

Rose Are you married?

Ralph No.

Rose Sorry. That was rather blunt.

Ralph We like that up here. Are you?

Rose Yes.

Ralph Kids?

Rose No.

Pause

More tea?

Ralph If I'm not in the way.

Rose Not a bit. Go on about being alone.

Ralph Do you think I'm talking daft?

Rose Far from it.

Ralph You know of Day Lewis? Not the film star. His dad.

Rose The poet laureate as was?

Ralph Yes. It's in *The Magnetic Mountain*. He's talking to his lover.

> "…There's but one room
> Of all the house you may never
> Share, deny or enter.
> There, as a candle's beam
> Stands firm and will not waver
> Spire-straight in a close chamber,
> As though in shadowy cave a
> Stalagmite of flame,
> The integral spirit climbs
> The dark in light for ever."

I believe that.

Rose Crikey. That's very good. Will you write it down for me?

Ralph Bit like the talking parrot, eh? The plumber who quotes poetry.

Rose Don't be silly. I've already apologised for that. I don't know why we're still such suckers for stereotypes. Just ghastly ingrained English snobbery, I suppose. Ludicrous for someone who thinks of herself as a painter. I mean, Hockney's never lost his Yorkshire, has he?

Ralph Nor Alan Bennett.

Rose Exactly. Actually, my husband's a poet.

Ralph Really? Will I have heard of him?

Rose Doubt it. He only publishes in small magazines. And not very often at that. Arthur Rawsthorne.

Ralph shakes his head

No, of course not. Mostly, his poetry's very private.

Ralph Won't make much of a living, then.

Rose Oh, he's a stockbroker. Financial adviser actually. Plays the money markets.

Ralph I never understand all that.

Rose To be honest, neither do I. But I know it's fairly hair-raising. He's living on his nerves most of the time. So, in private, he turns to poetry.

Ralph Sounds sensible.

Rose Oh, he is. Very sensible.

Ralph Are you sensible?

Rose Not often.

Ralph Then you must make a good mix.

Rose Yes, I think so.

Pause

Ralph Best be going.

Rose No hurry. You haven't finished your tea.

Ralph If you said it looked like snow——

Rose Is it far, where you live?

Ralph Only in the village. But this track can get cut off in heavy snow.

Rose Oh, these are only flurries. You still haven't really told me what going round the world did for you.

Ralph Taught me you can travel the longest journeys staying at home.

Rose Oh, you are a wise man, Mr Grayling.

Ralph Ralph.

Rose Ralph. I'm Rose.

Ralph We alliterate, then, Rose.

Rose We do do that, Ralph.

Pause

Do you live alone?

Ralph At the moment. Got a flat above the village Post Office. Mum and Dad aren't far. I go there for me Sunday dinner.

Rose Difficult not to be inquisitive when you meet someone for the first time, isn't it?

Ralph We could talk about the weather.

Rose We have a bit. What other walks should I do?

Ralph Been along the Wharfe to Burnsall?

Rose No.

Ralph Should do that, then. Got a good map?

Rose Ordnance Pathfinder.

Ralph You won't get lost, then.

Rose I love maps. I never understood them at school. The penny hadn't dropped. It was my husband who showed me. I remember saying to him in amazement "You mean if we turn left on the ground it's left on the map?"

Ralph Been married long?

Rose Nearly twenty years.

Ralph You don't look old enough.

Rose This is where I say flattery will get you nowhere. Does marriage figure in your plans at all?

Ralph (*after a pause*) Not with anyone I've met so far.

Rose But might it?

Ralph Oh, yes. You have this dream, don't you? The soul mate. Well ... you've got yours, I suppose.

Rose Yes... It's not always as romantic as that, but yes... Yes, I think we are ... soul mates... But there's still that room in the poem, isn't there? With the stalagmite. You will write it out for me, won't you?

Ralph I'll do it at home. Make sure I get it right. I'll leave it next the Aga.

Rose Thanks.

Long silence and finishing tea

Ralph I'll be off, then.

Rose Right.

Ralph (*nodding at the telly*) Do you watch that thing in the evenings?

Rose Only for the weather forecast. I've brought some good books.

Ralph I prefer books. I'll leave you in peace, then. Thanks for the tea.

Rose Thanks for the company.

Ralph Broken the retreat, have I?

Rose Oh, I'll give myself an extra penance.

Ralph Glad the Aga's working.

Rose Yes. I call her blessed Aga to be on the right side.

Ralph Household gods, eh? Like the Romans.

Rose Absolutely.

Ralph Goodbye, then.

Rose Goodbye, Mr Grayling.

Ralph Ralph.

Rose Ralph, of course.

Ralph Goodbye, Rose.

Ralph goes out

After he's gone, Rose clears the cups to the kitchen and then switches on the television

Rose Bugger. Missed the forecast. (*She switches it off again*) Get it at nine. (*She brings stuff in from the kitchen and starts thoughtfully preparing salad. After a few moments, she turns on the tape recorder*) Am I actually flirting? Is that what's going on? Is he? Can't get him out of my mind. Lost my cool somehow. I mean, it was all right while he was sitting there. I enjoyed it. Getting to know him. But looking back... I'm not sure how innocent it all was. There's something provoking about him. And yet ... something restful too. Oh, well. Probably never see him again. Mustn't let myself be side-tracked. I'm supposed to come out of this week with a decision, aren't I? Three possibilities. Put myself in the hands of the bloody doctors again and let them insert this tube thing. Put myself in the hands of different doctors and suffer the ghastly Buchenwald of chemotherapy. Or do nothing and *will* the lump away like I have all the others. To be or not to be. Or just to be... I've been shirking the issue, Sal. Just enjoying being here. The freedom. The beauty. The joy of it. Feeling so well. Full of the natural aches and pains of walking instead of all those imaginary ones you think are cancer popping up in new places. I'm looking like an advertisement for Horlicks. Nobody'd believe there was anything the matter with me. I bet Grayling doesn't. Ralph. Funny old-fashioned name. Quite suits him. (*She shakes her head*) Begone! So am I just sticking my head in the sand? That's not what you want me to do. Or Arthur. Not why I'm here. You both want me to take decisions for myself. But how can I when I feel so absolutely and completely well? I haven't choked once here. I know it's because I'm eating alone and undisturbed and can concentrate and take my time. Still, even the Centre doctors are advising me to have the damn thing put in. Buy yourself a breathing space, they say. Oh, dear. And if the only other alternative is chemotherapy... I've seen them sitting there in the waiting room. Grey hairless lumps of misery. Suspended in time. (*She pauses*) It's so consuming, this struggle, Sally. It kind of takes over your life. Doesn't leave much time for anything else. Hell, what am I saying exactly? Keeping myself alive doesn't leave time for living? Great. Can you sort that one out for me? Seven years ago we'd begun to think it was all a memory. Six-monthly check-ups had given way to annual ones. Life with one tit was becoming the norm. After all, much less incapacitating than one leg or one arm. So long as you're not a stripper you can carry on regardless. Nobody knew except Arthur and Liz and my sisters. And the occasional surprised dress-shop assistant. We'd settled down so completely we even allowed ourselves the luxury of domestic tiffs like ordinary married couples.

Provence Lighting up

Arthur Shall we go to Pierrot's tonight? Or that place on the front at Cassis?

Rose I thought I might cook in.

Arthur Do you really want to do that?

Rose There's masses of bits and pieces to finish up. I could do Rosie's Provençal Mess. You like that.

Arthur I like going out too.

Rose I shall enjoy cooking.

Arthur I know you will. But you can cook at home.

Rose Not with herbs from our own hillside. Not with popping down the lane for a bit of hand-picked fennel.

Arthur Just like to give you a break sometimes.

Rose It's very thoughtful of you, darling, but I actually get rather more fun pottering about in my own kitchen.

Arthur It's not your own kitchen.

Rose It feels like it after all these years.

Arthur You always say you like seeing the way they do things here.

Rose I do. But we were out last night. And the night before. Don't keep on about it.

Arthur It's holidays. We can't afford these kind of meals at home. In England you're paying for the crockery and the furniture and three sets of cutlery. Here you just pay for the food.

Rose Well, I still feel like cooking in.

Arthur We're out of wine.

Rose You can pop into the village.

Arthur They only have the local rosé.

Rose It's not that bad. I quite like it. We can't have Château-bottled every night.

Arthur Why can't we? Who's holding the purse-strings?

Rose (*after a pause*) That's a sore-ish point, isn't it? I could earn, if you'd let me.

Arthur Don't change the subject.

Rose I'm not. You brought up money.

Arthur No, you did. You said we couldn't afford Château-bottled every night.

Rose Well, I thought we couldn't.

Arthur On holiday, the sky's the limit.

Rose But you never tell me how high the sky is. How am I supposed to know? You just dole me out a wad of francs——

Arthur When I stop doling out will be the time to complain.

Rose Well, let's drop the subject.

Arthur We haven't reached a decision yet.

Rose Yes we have.

Arthur What is it?

Rose We're eating in.

Arthur That's not a decision: that's an ultimatum.

Rose Because it hasn't gone your way. You're a great democrat you are.

Arthur And you're an illogical prat. One vote to one is not a democratic victory.

Rose No. It's stalemate. I'm cooking in. You can share it if you like.

Pause. Rose is really quite disproportionately upset

Trouble with you, Arthur, is you've been spoiled all your life. First by your mother——

Arthur My mother never spoiled me——

Rose First by your mother and then by me.

Arthur Oh God, now we're really into cliché country.

Rose True enough. And the result is you never look outside yourself.

Arthur I? I never look outside myself? You can say that?

Rose I just said it.

Arthur Well! I'll spare you the enumeration of my virtues.

Rose Good. Oh, you're kind enough. You're naturally kind. You're aghast if you tread on a beetle. But the act of imagination that would actually involve you with other people—you're not up to that.

Arthur I'm tempted to say I can't believe my ears.

Rose Well, go on, give in. Say it.

Arthur I can't believe my ears.

Rose If you loved me, instead of just what I can be in your life like a sort of pet, you'd give in to me once in a way.

Arthur You mean we'd have a shoal of kids and stay home to dinner?

Rose Something like that.

Arthur Of all the bloody ungrateful——

Rose Oh, I know you've been gentle and made a lot of fuss of me since the operation. But I want respect as a person too. Respect as a painter. If I'm not to have a family, why can't I carry out the profession I was trained for?

Arthur You can paint as much as you like.

Rose That's not the same. You never encourage me to exhibit or treat me as a person who has her own ideas about how much we should spend and whether we should go out to dinner and if I want to make Provençal Mess you should bloody well encourage me.

Long pause. Rose starts to snivel

Arthur Oh, shit.

Pause. He takes her in his arms

Rose (*not resisting*) Leave me alone.

Arthur Not bloody likely.

Pause

Rose We'll go to that fucking place on the front at Cassis.

Arthur No, we'll stay in.

Rose Now we're both just capitulating. That's no bloody use. That's a
victory for neither of us.

Arthur Do we have to have victories?

Rose I'm a small principality. I need them sometimes.

Arthur You won the greatest.

Rose What? Oh, that.

Arthur Amazing, isn't it, that we can forget? I sometimes even find
myself wondering whether you ever had cancer.

Rose *You* didn't have to have the operation.

Arthur Maybe they mixed up the slides. That kind of thing's always
happening.

Rose We could sue. Make an enormous amount of money.

Arthur Good idea. What shall we spend it on?

Rose Well, first I could have my new exhibition.

Arthur We could have a new car.

Rose I like the old one.

Pause

Arthur So what are we doing, then?

Rose I said, first——

Arthur No, I mean tonight. In or out?

Rose Oh...

Arthur You need victories, so in.

Rose That wouldn't be a victory. Not now.

Pause

Arthur So Pierrot's or Cassis?

Rose I'll dowse for it. You write the names on bits of paper.

Arthur I'll put "home" in as well, to be fair. You won't cheat, will you?

Rose Scrunchle them up. Make it impossible.

*Arthur tears off three scraps of paper, and scribbles on them, rolls them
into balls, and places them before Rose. She takes the pendant from
around her neck and dowses over the scraps, letting it swing loosely from
the joint of her thumb*

Please tell us which we should do tonight. To the left for "no", for "yes"
to the right...

Arthur Hey, I'm the poet in this family.

Rose Shh... (*She repeats this incantation several times. The pendant finally gives a strong signal to the right. Rose thanks the pendant and kisses it*)

Arthur picks up the chosen scrap and unravels it

So which is it?

Arthur Well, I'll be buggered.

Rose Home?

Arthur Home.

Pause

I still feel like going out.

Rose I still feel like staying in.

Arthur Impasse.

Rose Yes. But you should accept the pendulum's decision.

Arthur You know what an unbeliever I am. Compromise: down the café for a drink first.

Rose No.

Brief pause

Down the café for a brandy afterwards.

Arthur Done.

They both start to laugh. They laugh more and more hysterically and end up in each other's arms

END OF ACT I

ACT II

The middle of the night

Rose comes downstairs and goes into the kitchen for a glass of water. She comes into the living-room and automatically switches on the tape recorder

Rose Can't sleep. Everything's tick, tick, tick. Good morning, Sally. It's the grey hours. Life at its lowest ebb. Probably the sort of time Mum gave up her ghost. I'm not dying. Just not sleeping either. Went out like a baby the first few nights. I suppose it's because it's all coming to an end and I'm no nearer a decision.

Tick, tick, tick. No good just lying up there thinking bad thoughts. I'll bring the story up to date.

Seven years ago. There was this flu bug going round with a nasty chesty finish to it. Everybody at the gallery went under. And I'd had my exhibition and it was a flop. I could feel waves of hate coming off the people as they looked at the stuff. Which was a new experience for me and not one I knew how to handle. My things had always been fairly popular, in a small way. But I'd gone off down new directions and nobody liked it. I tried to feel anonymous whenever I visited the gallery but it didn't work. I felt as if I was walking round in a smock with a paint brush in my hand. I tried staying away but that was worse. I had to be there. I had to see their hatred. I wanted to close down the exhibition after the reviews but Arthur wasn't having any. He'd spent good money on it, he said. Let it run its course. If artists wanted to communicate they must bear the consequences. "You'll probably have the last laugh. Think of Whistler." Well, I didn't want to think of Whistler. Or his mother. Or my mother. I was low, low, low.

So, of course, I caught the flu. Which turned into the chesty cough. But
mine was still racking me when everybody else's had gone away. After
about two months of it Arthur insisted I had a chest X-ray. And that was
it. There it was. "A shadow on the lungs." What do they bloody mean,
a shadow? I mean, shadows move, don't they? Pass over. Sun, cloud,
shadow, sun. Not this one. Grave faces. "About three months, Mrs
Rawsthorne." And that's when Arthur took charge and we fled to the
Cancer Help Centre. I suppose it's everybody's last resort, which is why
their recovery rate is not impressive. But immediately we crossed the
threshold we felt the difference. The love. There's no other word for it.
Not something you get in waves from the average hospital.

And I started to take myself in hand and do all the things prescribed.
Stuck rigidly to the diet. Learnt to meditate. To visualise. To think
positive. And amazingly the cough cleared up and I began to feel strong.
My consultant couldn't believe his eyes. He peered and peered at the
new X-ray willing it to be as bad as he'd expected but he couldn't. "It
seems, if anything, to be slightly less threatening, Mrs Rawsthorne."
You bloody bet it did. And I was determined it was going to go away
altogether. There'd been miracle cures in the past. Me too. Me too.

And so it seemed I was for nearly seven years. But they can't leave well
alone, can they? "You've done so well, Mrs Rawsthorne, you seem to
be held in such excellent balance, I think a change of drug might kill the
thing altogether." Because I'd been on a mild anti-cancer drug which he
of course thought was doing all the good work. Whereas I knew it was
me. Me. So OK. Let him change the drug. What harm? He'd had an
expensive training. He might even be right.

Provence Lighting up

*Arthur is helping Rose into the cottage. She is leaning on him heavily
and gasping for breath. He leads her to a chair. He is shaking with
worry*

Arthur God, Rose, you'll be all right, darling. We've made it, sweetheart.
We're home. God, I thought I'd never get you off the beach.
Rose (*gasping it out*) Must ... phone ... the Centre...
Arthur I'll get the number. Where's that bloody bit of paper? "Phoning
Home From Abroad". Do you remember where we put it?

Rose (*practical even in disaster*) By ... the telephone... I should think...

Arthur (*trying very hard not to flap*) Of course. Obvious. Yes. Here it is. Thank God for the Charge Card. (*He mutters as he reads*) Countries shown in red... France... call via BT Direct... (*He dials*) Hallo? Miraculous. A homely voice. ... Yes ... it's 086 736 30... Check number... 73. ... Yes, I want 01 998 892 7172... This is brilliant, Rose, I'm getting straight through. Who do you want, darling?

Rose Dr Elizabeth.

Arthur What's her other name?

Rose Doesn't matter ... they always ... use Christian names... (*Her breaths are coming in great life-searching gasps*)

Arthur (*into the phone*) Oh, hallo, can I speak to Dr Elizabeth, please? ... Arthur Rawsthorne. It's very urgent. About my wife Rose. ... Yes, of course I'll hang on, but I'm phoning from the south of France. (*To Rose*) Thank God she's in. They're paging her.

Rose gets up and staggers slowly to the phone. Arthur arranges a chair for her

(*Into the phone*) Is that Dr Elizabeth? ... Yes, Arthur Rawsthorne. We're in Provence on holiday and Rose has just had a terrible attack of breathlessness. I don't know if she'll be able to talk to you but she wants to try. I'll pass you on.

Rose (*into the phone; with difficulty*) Hallo, Elizabeth... I was swimming ... and then I couldn't get my breath... It's ghastly ... feels like the end... (*She listens*) Yes... Yes... (*After a pause*) Tell Arthur. (*She passes the receiver to Arthur*)

Arthur (*into the phone*) Hallo, Elizabeth. ... Yes. ... She's to stop taking the new pills at once? Right. ... It's water-retention you think? ... Yes, I'll try. Spell it out for me. (*He writes*) Do you think I'll be able to get it at a French pharmacie? ... Get a doctor to prescribe it? That won't be easy. ... What? ... We're about a dozen kilometres from Draguignan. ... Yes, I'll hang on. (*To Rose*) She's looking up in some medical *Who's Who* or other.

Pause. Waiting

(*Into the phone*) Yes, Elizabeth, I'm still here. (*To Rose*) God, what luck! She knows someone. Someone she met on a conference. (*Into the*

phone) Hang on, Elizabeth, I'm writing it down. Dr Claude Vallois. …
Two "l"s. … Yes. 17 bis, Rue de France, Draguignan. Phone… What?
… *You'll* phone? That's wonderful, Elizabeth. … What? … Just get in
the car and go. Right. Bless you, Elizabeth. … Yes, I'll call you tonight.
Rose has your home number? Yes, I'll call you tonight. Bye. (*He puts
the phone down and takes a deep breath*) OK, darling. Off we go. Little
spin to Draguignan. Dr Vallois to the rescue. (*He begins to help her out
to the car*) Come on, Rosie. One small step for mankind…

In Yorkshire it is still night

Rose Well, as you know, they got me out of that spin. Makes me think
someone's watching over me sometimes. As if I'm not meant to go yet.
They haven't got the room ready or something. I mean, of all the doctors
in the south of France, Elizabeth has to know one not ten miles away.
But it set me back a good seven years, I reckon. Clouds looming back
on the horizon. And now this other thing in my neck… Oh, God, it's so
boring. I just want to live and enjoy living. That's what was so
wonderful about the start of this week. Me and the lambs and the birds
and the bunnies. All alive and bonding. Taking part in the spring of the
year. (*She pauses*) I can't think any more. I can't decide. Someone's
going to have to tell me. Room ready or not. (*She pauses*) Know what,
Sally? When the first light comes I'm going to pack my rucksack and
go out for the day. Put it all behind me. Just live. Just be part of it all. For
another whole day. And no more talking to this bloody thing. (*She
switches to re-wind and pauses*) Just live.

Yorkshire Lighting changes to late afternoon

*Ralph stands transfixed in the empty room, listening, as the tape repeats
the last paragraphs and comes to an end*

*Just before it ends Rose comes in the door. She stands stock still staring
at him. A ghastly moment*

(*Outraged*) You've been listening?
Ralph (*stupidly*) The radio battery's down. I thought there might be some
music on it.
Rose (*tensely*) I don't believe it! That is extremely private and personal.

Ralph That flue was getting jammed up. I needed to rod it out.

Rose You shouldn't have listened. That's … dreadful… (*No words seem adequate*) Like listening at keyholes.

Ralph I thought there'd be music.

Rose How much have you heard?

Ralph I got interested. Like a radio play almost. I thought at first perhaps you were writing a play.

Rose (*looking at the machine*) You've listened to the whole fucking thing. That's my life in there.

Ralph Sorry…

Rose It's therapy. I'm talking to my counsellor. It's very personal.

Ralph Sorry. Forgot me place.

Rose And that's just bloody insensitive and rude.

Ralph Talking to your analyst.

Rose My counsellor.

Ralph Like Woody Allen.

Rose Not in the least like Woody Allen. I've got cancer.

Ralph Yes. I sort of gathered. I'm a bit muddled about the immediate situation.

Rose What business is it of yours?

Ralph None. Except no man is an island. For whom the bell tolls. All that.

Pause. They stare at one another, both equally appalled by the situation

The flue was getting jammed up again. I was going to rod it out. I thought I'd put on a bit of music.

Rose Well, I think you can go.

Ralph Yes. When I've rodded the flue.

Rose You haven't even done it?

Ralph I got interested.

Rose Of all the bloody cheek. You bastard!

Ralph I wasn't thinking of it as cheek. I just … couldn't stop listening.

Pause

You've got a lovely voice, Rose.

Rose Is that your idea of an apology?

Ralph I suppose I should apologise. It was nosey. But it didn't quite seem like anything bad. Just to listen.

Pause

I was appalled, actually.

Pause

I started out just listening—as it might be to a play or something. I was enjoying the sound of your voice. I didn't know what it was. Some of it seemed just like a diary.

Rose Exactly. How would you feel to come home and find a complete stranger reading your diary?

Ralph Put like that, it certainly doesn't seem right. If it had been a written diary, I'd have never... I'd have cut me throat sooner. But your voice ... and you sound so cheerful some of the time ... and then so depressed. Rose, I'm sorry. I'll rod the flue.

Rose I think that would be best, Mr Grayling.

Ralph A complete stranger?

Rose Certainly.

Ralph I thought we had quite a friendly chat.

Rose I'm friendly to my greengrocer.

Ralph Ah, yes. I must remember my place. I'm the man who does the Aga.

Rose Oh, God. Can't you see I'm very upset?

Ralph Of course I can. Can't you see I am?

Rose So you should be.

Ralph I don't mean because I listened. I mean because of what I heard.

Pause. He moves toward the kitchen

I'll rod the flue.

Rose I feel all mucky. As if I'd caught you rummaging in my underwear.

Ralph Not as bad as that, surely? There's nothing mucky on that tape.

Rose It's your listening that's mucky.

Ralph I'm sorry. I'm very sorry, Mrs Rawsthorne. I'll rod the flue.

Rose Rose.

Ralph Rose. I'm sorry, Rose. Oh, listen, bugger the flue, can't we talk about it?

Rose What?

Ralph You. What's happening to you.

Rose Why?

Pause

Ralph comes back into the room

Ralph No man is an island. We're all part of the main.

Rose You can spare me the Dean of St Paul's.

Ralph Just says it all, somehow. Still, I'll try and put it in me own words.

Rose Don't bother.

Ralph You said on the tape were we flirting.

Rose Christ!

Ralph I don't think that's the right word for it. But since the other day I've kept on seeing you in my mind. And you said something the same. It's like … it's like unfinished business in a way.

Rose Listen, Ralph, all we did was we sat at this table and we drank a cup of tea and had a chat.

Ralph We exchanged names.

Rose That was perhaps foolish. I'm not alone very often. I probably behaved foolishly.

Ralph I don't think so. When I thought of you, I thought of you as a new friend.

Rose We know absolutely nothing about each other.

Ralph You know nothing about me.

Rose Oh, yes, of course. The confessional. Well, that just makes me feel worse.

Ralph I'd quite like to square it up. Tell you about me.

Rose I'm not sure I'm interested. Unless you've got cancer.

Ralph No. I haven't got cancer. Is that all you're interested in? People who've got cancer?

Rose It does become an obsession. We all cling together.

Ralph That's understandable. But be better if you each clung to someone who's whole.

Rose I do. My husband.

Pause

Ralph I don't want to say anything against him.

Rose Good. I should bloody think not.

Ralph He's stood by you.

Rose He certainly has.

Pause

Ralph But ... in a way ... unless I've got the wrong end of the stick...
Rose I'm sure you have.
Ralph He's only making amends like. There's been damage done.
Rose Are you a psychiatrist?
Ralph Professionally, no.
Rose Please go, Mr Grayling. I'm not going to discuss my married life with a complete stranger.
Ralph You discuss it with her.
Rose Miss Goodwin is not a complete stranger. She's a professional counsellor.
Ralph I think Sally's smashing. She doesn't treat me like the odd job man either. She'll often meet me down the *Mason*'s for a pint. I think she'd say we're friends. You can ask her.
Rose I'm not really interested.
Ralph You're just interested in yourself?
Rose I have to be...

Pause

Ralph I'll rod the flue.
Rose I shouldn't bother. I'm leaving tomorrow anyway.
Ralph Just here for the week?
Rose Yes. Let's just forget this whole beastly incident, shall we, and say goodbye.

Pause

Ralph I'd rather not.

Pause

Just yet.
Rose If you're going to be a nuisance——
Ralph You'll what? Send for my mate Constable Yardley?
Rose Doesn't it strike you that you're being rather unkind?
Ralph No. I'm trying to be kind. It's a good word. Kindness. If you think about it.

Rose Well, I can do without a sympathetic pat from you.

Ralph Now who's being unkind?

Rose When you've got cancer you don't have to be kind.

Ralph Is that so? Lets you off being human, does it?

Rose Please go. I'm tired. And upset. And I've got to think about packing.

Ralph What time you going tomorrow?

Rose My husband's picking me up in the afternoon.

Ralph Could we go for a walk tomorrow morning?

Rose You and me?

Ralph Yes.

Rose What ever for?

Ralph I just fancy it.

Rose Well, I don't think I owe you any favours, Mr Grayling.

Ralph Back to "Mr" again, are we?

Rose Just please bloody go.

Ralph Wouldn't like us to part enemies. I don't think that'd be good for either of us. You'd possibly fret.

Rose You flatter yourself.

Ralph I've a fancy to show you the trout farm. And the lambing. I know you're interested in that. I've got friends lambing right now. We could watch.

Rose Oh, just bugger off.

Ralph Tell you what. I'll knock on the door about nine. In case you've changed your mind. If you don't come out, no harm done. I won't knock twice.

Pause

You're sure you don't want me to rod the flue?

Rose Quite sure. Absolutely flaming positive.

Ralph Right. (*He goes to the door*) Goodbye, Rose.

Pause

Sleep tight.

Rose Some hopes.

Ralph Oh, go on, you can cry yourself to sleep.

Rose Your kindness is overwhelming.

Ralph I hope so. Bye.

Ralph goes out

Rose leans forward with her head on her arms and sobs

The next day. For a moment or two the room is empty

We hear voices and even laughter from outside

Rose and Ralph enter

Rose There's not much to eat apart from salad.
Ralph We should have gone round by the pub.
Rose I've got some wine.
Ralph That'll do. Particularly as it's "good" wine.

Pause

Rose Yes...

Pause

I was almost about to thank you for not mentioning any of that.
Ralph It wasn't a problem. We had plenty to see.
Rose Yes... (*Pouring the wine*) Amazing to think they send all those poor
     fish back up to Scotland to spawn.
Ralph So they can sell it as Scottish salmon.
Rose What a fraud. All their formative influences are Yorkshire ones.
Ralph Like mine.
Rose Did you never think of leaving?
Ralph I went round the world.
Rose I meant when you came back.
Ralph No reason. Cheers.
Rose Cheers.

Pause

The lambs were so sweet.
Ralph I wonder why it is women go all soggy over lambs?
Rose Not just women. William Blake.

Ralph Don't know much about him. Bit of a nutter, wasn't he?

Rose Eccentric. He and his wife used to sit in their garden stark naked pretending to be Adam and Eve.

Ralph Doesn't sound so daft.

Rose "Little lamb who made thee?" And Wordsworth. "The spring lambs bound as to the tabor's sound."

Ralph Ah. You never hear them go on so about sheep. You know lots of poetry.

Rose No more than you. That Day Lewis was sensational.

Ralph Is it good being married to a poet?

Pause

OK, no need to answer. It was a totally innocent question.

Pause

Will I like him? Arthur?

Rose I'd rather you weren't here when he comes.

Ralph Why?

Rose Well—I'm supposed to be on retreat, remember?

Ralph The jealous type, is he?

Rose I wouldn't know. He's never had cause.

Ralph Well, he still hasn't.

Rose I'd still rather…

Ralph Right.

Pause

So will I never see you again?

Rose I suppose I might come back. If all goes well.

Ralph On your own?

Rose Does it matter?

Ralph Does to me.

Rose I think you're being rather silly.

Ralph I expect I am. You enjoyed this morning, though, didn't you?

Rose Yes, of course.

Ralph I'm glad you came. Wasn't sure you would.

Rose Neither was I. In fact, I answered the door without thinking.

Ralph But you came.

Rose It would have seemed childish not to.

Ralph Got your packing done?

Rose Pretty well, yes. Just the kitchen stuff but that can go loose in the car.

Ralph Those shiny saucepans all yours?

Rose Yes.

Ralph Thought I didn't recognize them.

Rose I have to cook in steel saucepans. Aluminium contaminates.

Ralph God, it's like space travel, isn't it? The hygiene. What's that other big thing?

Rose My juice extractor. I drink a pint of carrot juice a day.

Ralph Can't be bad.

Rose It isn't. Nicer than diet coke. But it takes a hell of a time to prepare. In fact, the whole diet's bloody time-consuming, which, when you may not have very much time left in the first place… Sorry. I didn't intend to refer to any of that.

Ralph Don't you think it's quite painful, avoiding it? Like trying not to look someone in the eye who's got a squint.

Rose If it were only that.

Ralph Rose, don't get angry at what I'm going to say. But I know so much you might as well tell me the rest.

Rose I haven't played back any of that tape. I can't remember what you know and what you don't.

Ralph Well, you could give me the bald clinical history. I mean Sally Goodwin knows so much you sort of skip the details. And half the time I was too stunned to take them in.

Rose Well … start from what you know.

Ralph It's a bit indelicate, isn't it?

Rose You mean I had my breast off?

Ralph nods

That long ago ceased to embarrass. Guess which.

He blushes

You soon learn not to be shy about it. Arthur helped me with that. He had me sunbathing within six months.

Ralph I'm not your husband.

Rose You wanted to know. That's where it started. The classic lump in the breast. No bigger than a pimple. But it turned out to be malignant so they wanted the whole thing off. That gives you nightmares. You wonder what they've done with it. Can you imagine? I mean can you imagine one of the most intimate parts of you being carted out in a bucket? Can you imagine your cock in a bucket, Ralph? Sorry, but you wanted this.

Ralph You're giving me that ache in the groin. Do women get that?

Rose We get enough aches. Then, a few months later, lumps appeared under my armpits. "Secondaries" is the technical term. In the lymph gland. Very usual if the op's been done too late. The thing spreads like something in a sci-fi movie. So those had to come out. Followed by a course of radiotherapy which really zombies you. And, after that… I was completely clear for seven glorious years. You soon come to accept there's a bit of you missing. Especially if your husband pretends not to notice any difference.

Pause

Ralph So then you got this flu and this cough?

Rose Yes. And the X-ray showed up a shadow on the lungs.

Ralph Lung cancer it was now?

Rose Yes. I tell you, it runs around like a cornered mouse.

Ralph But you said the X-rays were better.

Rose The X-rays were a bloody miracle. I was a bloody miracle.

Ralph This is what you do for yourself, is it? What they call alternative?

Rose Yes, that's what the Centre's mainly about. Although they have qualified doctors too. And more and more of the top specialists are coming to see the point.

Ralph What do you do, exactly?

Rose Oh, Ralph, it'd take too long. And you probably wouldn't believe me either. It can be very exhausting, trying to convince people.

Ralph We'll put a time limit on it. Like a game. See what you can do in five minutes.

Rose Three.

Ralph Done.

Rose Most cancers have an emotional origin.

Ralph So you find out what's bugging you and the lumps go away?

Rose Who's telling this?

Ralph Just helping.

Rose There's rather more to it than that. You have to change your whole way of thinking. Get rid of anything negative. There's a saying— "Energy follows thought". So the moment you catch yourself having a negative thought——

Ralph Give me an example.

Rose Er... "Damn. I always choose the wrong queue at the supermarket check-out."

Ralph Yes, so do I. What do you change that to?

Rose Er... How nice not to have to hurry.

"What is this life if, full of care
We have no time to stand and stare..."

Ralph (*laughing*) And that makes you better?

Rose Energy follows thought. Have you ever heard of creative visualisation?

Ralph No.

Rose I could teach you how to get rid of a cold, for instance. Visualise it away.

Ralph Tell.

Rose Well, colds generally start in the throat, don't they? So at the first signs you sit down somewhere quiet and imagine—say, a fountain spraying in your throat. A fountain of clear spring water washing it clean. Flooding all the passages around. For about twenty minutes.

Pause

Ralph And that's all?

Rose I haven't had a cold in seven years.

Ralph So you imagine things about this mouse. Where is he now?

Rose Little lumps keep springing up all over the place. You know, a bit like you press something down and it pops up somewhere else. They're only about the size of a garden pea. Not even that. A mange-tout. There's one in my stomach. Been there for years. Doesn't move. Doesn't grow. But then, about a year ago, I noticed one in my neck. And lately it's grown bigger and it's pressing on my oesophagus.

Ralph And that's why you have difficulty in swallowing and you choke sometimes?

Rose Yes.

Ralph And the visualisations and things—they aren't working any more?

Rose Not noticeably.

Ralph So the things they can do ... the official doctors ... that's what you've come away to think about?

Rose Yes.

Ralph But you can't decide?

Rose No.

Pause

There. That's it. Three minutes.

Pause

It was nice not having to think about it all morning. I'd like never to have to think about it again.

Pause

Ralph I know you said you weren't interested in people who haven't got cancer——

Rose I was angry—exaggerating——

Ralph But I'd like you to know something about me now. It's a short story and not very exciting but I didn't want you to run off thinking I was some sort of ladies' man. I'm usually quite shy. I've only ever been in love once properly. This girl I met in Australia. We travelled across half the world together until she finally left me in New York.

Rose Why?

Ralph She didn't want to come any further. You see, it was a bit of an odd relationship. She was afraid of men. She'd been raped when she was sixteen. She made me into a sort of brother figure. Never let me sleep with her. And she wouldn't marry either. She was somehow stuck in sixteen, like Sleeping Beauty. I couldn't wake her up, try as I might.

Pause

It was a useless, dead-end relationship, and it wore me out, I can see that now. But I did love her.

Rose You just left her on her own in New York?

Ralph No, I put her on an aircraft back home. Home was part of the problem. It was a cocoon. One she didn't even want to break out of.

Rose How sad.

Ralph It was. She'd be very loving if only she'd let herself. Perhaps I was the wrong man. Too safe in a way. She was too safe with me.

Rose I bet Sally could have sorted her out.

Ralph I didn't know Sally then. So... That was the love of my life so far. I mean I've had girlfriends. I'm not a monk. But she was the only one who ... "engaged" me ... if you see what I mean...

Rose I think you're a bit of a crusader, Ralph. You look for causes.

Ralph Perhaps. I'm a sucker for vulnerability.

Rose And you find me vulnerable?

Ralph Oh, yes.

Rose But I'm not available, Ralph. I'm happily married. It'd be as frustrating as your Sleeping Beauty.

Pause

Ralph Are you being absolutely truthful?

Rose Of course.

Pause

Ralph You say I'm a crusader. I say you make the best of things. I've heard you, remember. Arthur said an unforgiveable thing to you—before you were ill—he said something like your mother was drinking you to death in her womb.

Rose They hated each other. They were jealous. I couldn't handle it.

Ralph If he loved you, he should have tried to love her.

Rose That's simplistic nonsense, Ralph. You can't choose who you hate and who you love.

Ralph Hate's irrational.

Rose Isn't love?

Ralph No, I don't think so. Not real love.

Rose Oh, come on. It's an emotion.

Ralph There's infatuation. I'm not talking about that.

Rose You can't control it.

Ralph I had to control mine for Emily.

Rose Well you're a bloody saint and martyr. And a fool to yourself. And anyway, how many men love their mothers-in-law? It's a music hall joke.

Ralph Times change. The music halls are gone for a start. I'd have tried to love her.

Rose Well bully for you. It's an easy thing to say, Ralph. She was drunk and destructive and vicious and bitchy every evening of her life and remembered absolutely nothing of it in the morning when she was nice middle-class Mrs Plumridge sitting at the breakfast table seriously doing *The Times* crossword.

Ralph OK, let's leave your mother. Why does Sally distrust him?

Rose She doesn't.

Ralph You ask her not to.

Rose It's nothing. It's a slight thing. They just don't get on very well. But Arthur admires Sally. He wants me to listen to her. He encourages me to see her.

Ralph He doesn't want to lose you.

Rose Well, thanks for admitting it.

Ralph He needs you.

Rose We need each other.

Ralph Why doesn't he like you to cry?

Rose Did you like Emily to cry?

Ralph I didn't like it but if she wanted to I let her. She cried a lot. It was necessary for her. She cried all night sometimes. When I said last night you'd cry yourself to sleep you thought I was being cruel, didn't you? That was naïve of you, Rose. I wanted you to cry.

Rose Am I supposed to be grateful?

Ralph If you'd stop giving smart answers and think about it for a minute … yes. And why doesn't he want you to paint?

Rose Of course he wants me to paint.

Ralph But not professionally.

Rose There's not much money in it, for God's sake. I'm not David Hockney. Arthur pays for my exhibitions.

Ralph Puts you on trial more like.

Rose I think I've had enough of this, Ralph. You're taking a wickedly unfair advantage of things you heard that weren't meant for your ears.

Ralph I can't un-hear them. What about the child you wanted?

Rose Stop! Stop right now! Do you hear? Stop!

Pause. Silence

Ralph Sometimes you meet someone … it was the same with Emily … and you just know.

Rose It didn't work with Emily.

Ralph She wasn't ready. May never be ready. It sort of half worked. We had that direct line to each other. But she was all jammed up with what had happened to her at sixteen and by how her family had cocooned her ever since. I couldn't fight past that.

Rose In *Sleeping Beauty*, the prince hacks his way through the undergrowth.

Ralph Yes. But suppose his kiss had only half woken her?

Rose It'd be a different story.

Ralph Yes. No happy ending.

Rose There can't be to this one either, Ralph.

Ralph Are you so sure?

Rose Haven't I made it clear to you how much Arthur means to me? How bound together we are?

Ralph Aye, but are they silken ropes or chains?

Rose My, we are being fanciful. Life ain't a fairy story, Ralph.

Ralph There was something on that tape somewhere about singing your own song.

Rose That was a visiting American guru at the Centre. Very ancient and wise. It was his catch-phrase. He said our business in life was to sing our own song. Not anybody else's. Find out what it was and sing it and we'd all be cured.

Ralph Did he produce any testimonials?

Rose Plenty. There was this big Wall Street banker whose boyhood dream had been to run away to sea. He had terminal cancer. Jacked in a multi-million dollar job and went off as a ship's steward. Ten years ago. As far as I know he's still alive and collecting his tips.

Ralph So what's your song, Rose?

Rose If only I knew.

Ralph Is Arthur helping you to find it?

Rose It's something you have to find for yourself.

Ralph If you'd never met Arthur, what would you have done?

Rose That's silly. That's fiction, not fact.

Ralph Well, pretend.

Rose I honestly don't know, Ralph. He's been everything to me. Lover—he was my first and only—mentor, guide … comforter … fun-friend…

Ralph Why doesn't he want children?

Rose It's too late now. Not worth discussing.

Ralph Is it? Didn't you say you could still conceive?

Rose Wouldn't be very responsible, would it?

Ralph Perhaps singing your own song is about being irresponsible. Anyway, why didn't he?

Rose I don't know exactly.

Ralph When you married him you naturally thought he would.

Rose We never talked about it... I suppose I assumed ... it's the norm ... two point four kids.

Ralph So why?

Rose I don't know.

Ralph I do. It's because he's a selfish bastard and you were quite right when you said he couldn't involve himself with other people.

Rose (*getting up*) Right. That's it. Time's up, Mr Grayling. Out.

Ralph (*taking hold of her*) Rose...

Rose (*struggling*) Let go of me ... how dare you...

Ralph Rose...

Rose (*fighting a gradually more unresisting fight*) Oh, God...

Ralph Rose...

Rose Oh, God...

Ralph Rose...

Rose (*now quite relaxed in his arms*) Oh, God...

Fade to black

Later

Rose is alone and on the phone

Yes, I've done all that, but look, Sal, I've got a favour to ask you. ... Well... I need more time. Can I stay on for a bit? ... Oh, you're an angel. ... Sort of unfinished business. ... Yes ... something I'm in the middle of. Well, it could be nothing, could be something ... but I need time ... to find out. ... No, I'm not lonely. I'll send the tape with Arthur so you'll sort of see... Yes, and ring me if you think anything important's come to the surface. But I think it's all the usual guff. ... Yes, I know I should. ... No, the swallowing's fine. Everything's under control. ... What? ... Well, right, perhaps not everything. But I'm working on it. ... You want me to make another tape? Blimey. I shall run out of things to think. You OK? ... Great. ... Well... Yes, I will, and you take care too. Bless you, Sally. Bye now.

She puts the phone down and stares into space. Then puts a new tape into the recorder and switches on

Hallo, Sally. Tape fucking two. I've just put down the phone from you. And for the first time I've lied to you. Feel bad about that. And I'm going to lie to Arthur too. Feel even worse about that. I'm just about to make a complete fucking idiot of myself—hence all the bad language. But you only live once, so they say, oh yes indeedy, I can't believe all that reincarnation bit, and anyway, what use would it be to me to come back as an antelope? And some of us not so long as others. My syntax is buckling under the strain, Sally. And my heart is banging like it hasn't since I was about fourteen and in love with the gym mistress. Is that a good sign of life? Increase the pumping rate? Sing your own song...? Don't know... Might not be mine... Don't know... If it is, I hope you'll all join in the chorus.

She hears a car draw up

Visitors. (*She turns off the tape and opens the door*)

Arthur enters

Arthur Gosh, you're looking smashing!
Rose I've been out a lot.
Arthur Stunning! And so well. You look about ten years younger.
Rose You're always saying that. I must have reached single figures by now.
Arthur No, you really do.
Rose I feel pretty good. How have you been?
Arthur Fine. Absolutely fine. Jenny and Richard gave me dinner on Wednesday.
Rose That was nice.
Arthur Relieved the monotony.
Rose How's the cooking been?
Arthur The "heating up" you mean? No problems. Gas four for twenty minutes: that sort of thing.
Rose I should have rung you earlier.
Arthur I'm here now.
Rose I mean, I should have tried to stop you coming.

Arthur looks surprised

I need longer. I need another week.

Pause

Arthur I see... Yes, I wish you had then. It's a pig of a drive.
Rose Yes, it was selfish: I'm sorry. Actually, I didn't really make up my mind until today, and by then it was too late to stop you. I've rung Sally. She says I can have the cottage.
Arthur Well, at least I can stay for the weekend.

Pause. Rose looks dubious

You mean that will break the retreat?
Rose You know the whole idea was to be alone.
Arthur For a week.
Rose Turns out not to be long enough.
Arthur There isn't all that time to waste if we want to get in the operation queue.
Rose But that's just what I haven't decided yet.

Pause

Arthur Surely it won't hurt for me to be here for the weekend?
Rose I suppose so...
Arthur Well... What a welcome. There was I thinking you might even be glad to see me.
Rose Of course I am. (*She pulls herself together*) I'm sorry. Yes, of course you can. What am I saying? Of course you can.
Arthur Actually, it'd only be tonight. I have to be in the office on Monday.
Rose Everything all right?
Arthur The usual nightmare. Busy as ever. Provence will be even more welcome this year. How's the swallowing?
Rose Been no trouble at all.
Arthur Filled your tape?
Rose Yes. I told Sally you'd take it back to her.
Arthur Can do.

Rose You wouldn't listen to it, would you?

Arthur Rose. Honestly! That's all between you and Sally.

Rose You might have been curious. Might have popped it in the cassette to while away the M1.

Arthur I'm half way through *The Magic Flute*.

Rose You're not curious?

Arthur Listen, the whole point of counselling is that it's a one-to-one relationship.

Rose Not always. Sally says we could have joint counselling.

Arthur Well, we don't need to, do we?

Rose Would you be afraid of it?

Arthur Of course not. Just be pointless. We've no secrets, have we?

Rose Have you?

Arthur None that I can think of. I may have broken the washing machine but I was going to confess that anyway.

Pause

I haven't brought a thing with me. Wash bag or clean undies or anything. I'll have to borrow your toothbrush. And you'll have to enjoy me tomorrow with designer stubble.

Rose Yes. Look, I have to go out. I have to get some things from the village to feed you.

Arthur I'll run you in.

Rose No, I'd rather walk.

Arthur I'll come with you. Could do with a stretch.

Rose No, I want to go alone.

Pause

Arthur Rose … What is it?

Rose Nothing, why?

Arthur You're not exactly behaving naturally.

Rose No, I'm not, am I? It's no good, Arthur. I can't hide anything from you. I don't even want to.

Pause

I've met someone.

Long pause

Arthur You mean you're having an affair?
Rose Well, it's not exactly got that far, I wouldn't say.
Arthur Who is he?
Rose A friend of Sally's. He came to mend the Aga.
Arthur Good grief. Lady Chatterley's lover.
Rose Don't be ridiculous.

Pause

  Well, I've told you.
Arthur And that's why you want to stay?
Rose Yes.
Arthur And me to go.
Rose It won't change anything between us.
Arthur I see.
Rose Are you very angry?
Arthur Just a bit stunned. It's been bloody quick. When did you meet
  him?
Rose Wednesday. The Aga was smoking——
Arthur I'm not bothered about the Aga. It's obviously not smoking any
  more.
Rose He mended it. It was the flue. He rodded it.
Arthur Rose, darling, I don't think I want details.
Rose I'll do whatever you say, Arthur. If you tell me to come home, I'll
  come.
Arthur And regret it and blame me ever after? You wanted to be off down
  the village to warn him I was staying?

Pause. Rose looks down

  You're expecting him tonight.
Rose God, it does seem sordid. Now you're here. Tell me not to be a
  bloody fool and come home.
Arthur That's something you must tell yourself.
Rose I can't. Bully me. Be masterful.
Arthur Beat you up even?
Rose I probably deserve it.

Arthur Rose, Rose, Rose... I love you, Rose.

Rose You're honestly not angry?

Arthur Not angry. Something much more complicated than that. What if I'd confessed something like that to you?

Rose I don't know. Is there anyone?

Arthur You know there isn't.

Rose It's so bloody unfair.

Arthur So's cancer. I suppose... (*Carefully*) I suppose it might even be right for you. Sally might think so. Might be just what you need.

Pause

Rose (*rather dolefully*) Why are you so good to me? What have I done to deserve it?

Arthur Been good to me. Can I have a cup of tea before I go?

Rose You do trust me, don't you? To come back to you?

Arthur What else?

Pause

Rose Exactly. What else?

There is the sound of a car

Arthur Who the hell's that?

Rose My God, it's him! Oh, Lord.

Arthur I'm not going to hide, Rose.

They wait awkwardly

   Ralph comes in

Ralph I saw the car. I'm Ralph Grayling.

Arthur Arthur Rawsthorne.

They don't shake hands

Ralph I don't know if Rose has said anything about me——

Arthur She said you'd been to mend the Aga.

Rose (*to Ralph*) I've told him.

Ralph It seemed dishonest not to come and meet you—although Rose didn't want me to. I mean, it's easy to deceive people you never see. I thought perhaps if I said hallo I might forget the whole thing.

Rose What??

Ralph Not what I feel for Rose. I mean doing anything about it.

Rose Do I have any say in this?

Arthur It certainly makes it more awkward for me. I could just about cope with the idea of a mystery lover. I don't know whether I'm bold enough to confront one in the flesh.

Rose Arthur's been bloody marvellous about it.

Ralph And I don't know whether I'm brazen enough to cope with the husband's encouragement.

Rose What—About—Me?

Arthur Yes, I think it's Rosie's decision.

Rose You make it sound like choosing wallpaper! For God's sake, I'm not choosing between you! I'm just deciding to stay on for a week.

Arthur With him.

Rose Yes. Unless he's backing out.

Ralph No. Just felt a bit of a shit. Towards your husband.

Rose I thought that was my privilege.

Arthur Well, while you're both deciding who's the biggest shit I think perhaps I'll just push off. It's a long drive. I'll get a cuppa on the way. Rose has my blessing. I don't think you'll expect one as well, will you? Goodbye, darling. (*With a wry smile*) Next Saturday, same time?

Rose Oh, Arthur… Why won't you tell me to come with you?

Arthur I think this is too important a moment in your life for me to boss you about.

Rose (*to Ralph*) You see? You see what he's like? Now do you believe me?

Arthur Been slagging me off, has he? What on earth have you been telling him?

Rose Nothing. Nothing but good.

Ralph It's a fancy gesture. I think if it were me, I'd fight for her.

Arthur Would you? I thought you came in half prepared to drop your suit?

Ralph I mean, if I were in your place.

Arthur No, I don't feel like that. There are different kinds of love, aren't there? Look, I'd much rather we hadn't met. I think it was crass of you. But I want Rose to cram her life to the full and if that for a week includes you, Amen. It might help her to get all sorts of things straight in her mind. So far there have been no villains in this pantomime—apart from the doctors, and they're more like the brokers' men. So let's please not create any now. The only villain is the cancer and the more heroes we can conscript the better.

Pause

So saying, he left. Bye Rosie, darling. I hope...

Pause

Rose What?

Arthur (*with a laugh*) I was going to say I hope it comes up to expectations, but that sounds a bit snide. Just ... take care ... be good ... really mean that. (*He kisses her brow*)

She remains motionless

(*To Ralph*) But I do want her back in one piece. (*To Rose*) Till next week, then.

Rose (*faintly*) Drive carefully.

Arthur Will do.

Rose Enjoy *The Magic Flute*.

Arthur I always do.

Arthur goes out

We hear the car start up and drive away

Rose You didn't have a lot to say for yourself. After that magnificent entrance.

Ralph Felt a fool.

Rose You're so bloody noble. You're both so bloody noble, you've both succeeded in making me feel like the tart for all seasons.

Ralph Rose...

Rose Oh, Rose, Rose, Rose. What do you all expect to get from chanting my name? Oh, God, now what have I done? Why couldn't you have waited? You've changed everything. It's just a farce now.

Ralph Isn't it better that we won't be cheating him?

Rose But of course we'll be cheating him! What about my marriage vows?

Ralph Don't you remember what the Church says the purpose of marriage is?

Rose To have and to hold, from this day forward——

Ralph No, not that bit. "First, it was ordained for the procreation of children, to be brought up in the fear and nurture of the Lord." Arthur cheated you on that. The mutual help and comfort thing is down number three on the list. I learned that a long time ago.

Rose Whatever for?

Ralph To remind me whenever I was in danger of taking it too lightly.

Rose I bet that's not even any longer in the prayer book.

Ralph Should be.

Rose And anyway, you and I are not going upstairs to get children, are we? Don't be crass. Arthur said you were crass and you are.

Ralph Love makes you a bit foolish, I suppose.

Rose And don't generalise. Love makes you foolish, perhaps.

Ralph I'm sorry.

Rose What a bloody muddle. And I thought this was going to help me.

Pause

Ralph Rose, I think we both need a little time on our own to get ourselves together. I'll go away now and come back later. With a very good bottle of wine.

Rose Just a minute. You said to Arthur, perhaps if you met him you might be able to forget the whole thing.

Ralph I meant if he really turned out to be the great guy you cracked him up to be——

Rose And didn't he?

Ralph It's hard to tell in ten minutes.

Rose And you would have thrown me over just like that? That's your idea of love?

Ralph Only if it seemed to be for your own good.

Rose Honestly! You're like a couple of doting parents deciding which medicine is best for me. I've had quite enough medicine. What I was looking forward to was a great roaring fuck with a comparative stranger.

Ralph Rose, please...

Rose Shocking you, am I? Good.

Ralph Maybe I was thick. I'm in as much of a muddle as you. I've never committed adultery before.

Rose A couple of hours ago it was love. Now it's adultery.

Ralph I can't seem to be able to say anything right.

Rose That's certainly true.

Ralph Forgive me.

Rose No. No, I can't forgive you. You take me up on this high mountain and show me all these goodies, like the bloody devil you are, and then they turn out to be a fucking mirage.

Ralph Rose...

Rose And stop saying my name. I'm beginning not to recognize it. If you don't like me saying fuck you've only yourself to blame. I don't often say it. I hardly ever say it. But I feel like saying it now. Fuck, fuck, fuck.

Ralph (*attempting to encompass her*) Darling——

Rose No, no, go away. Buy the wine. Buy at least four bottles. That's what I need. Anaesthesia.

Pause

Ralph (*turning at the door*) Do you prefer red or white?

Rose Two of each.

Ralph goes out

Rose doesn't know whether to laugh or cry. She goes to the phone and riffles through the papers by it. She dials a number

Hallo? Jeff's Taxis? ... Yes, I'd like one in about half an hour please. ... Stone Cottage, Ansell's Farm, Upper Burdon. It's just beyond—you know it? Miss Goodwin, that's right. ... I'm her friend, Mrs Rawsthorne. ... Well ... where's the nearest airport? Leeds/Bradford? ... How far is that? ... That'll be fine. Will you take a credit card? ... Great. (*With a laugh*) I can manage some cash for the tip. ... No, I don't know the time of the flight. When we get there will do. ... Yes, thank you very much. See you then. (*She puts down the phone and switches on the tape recorder*) Flight, Sally. Literally and figuratively. Ignominious flight. Doesn't matter where. Costa Brava or Belfast. Wherever the next plane goes to.

I tried to sing my own song, didn't I? I really tried.
But it was in the wrong key.

So I just feel like pulling up my roots.
Will I shriek, like the mandrake?
Choke to death over a plastic tray on the plane?
Have sex with a tall dark steward in the toilet?
Just read a good book?

I know one thing. I don't want to be messed about
with any more. Tubes, lasers, forget it. Even
counsellors, bless you.

Just tell everyone, including Arthur, that I've gone
on holiday.

I'll probably be back.

If I don't turn into a stalagmite.

END OF PLAY

FURNITURE AND PROPERTY LIST

Further dressing may be added at the director's discretion

ACT I

On stage: Wrapped-up easel
Wrapped-up canvases (including an abstract)
Wrapped-up brushes and paints
Comfy chair
Armchair
Chair
Bed
Phone
Note paper
Leaflet "Phoning Home From Abroad"
Hand-written list
Bottle of white wine
Glass
Calendar on the wall
Tea things
Television

Off stage: Suitcases, steel saucepans, books (**Arthur**)
Tape recorder (**Arthur**)
Bathing towel (**Arthur**)
Book (**Arthur**)
Lunch things (**Rose**)
Travel goods (**Arthur**)
Butterfly books (**Rose** and **Arthur**)
Salad things (**Rose**)

Personal: **Ralph:** business card, handkerchief
Rose: pendant

ACT II

On stage: As before

Off stage: Glass of water (**Rose**)

LIGHTING PLOT

Property fittings required: nil
One interior setting throughout

ACT I

To open: Yorkshire (slate-grey background) lighting

Cue 1   **Rose**: "And the deep nights with the stars."   (Page 5)
        Begin to change lighting to Provence (kingfisher-blue
          background): star-filled night effect

Cue 2   **Rose**: "Pool of tears."   (Page 5)
        Lighting change to Provence complete

Cue 3   **Arthur** ambles slowly out of sight   (Page 8)
        Change lighting to Yorkshire

Cue 4   **Rose**: "I also know he loves me."   (Page 9)
        Change lighting to Provence

Cue 5   **Rose**: "Wish it wasn't her car though."   (Page 10)
        Change lighting to Yorkshire

Cue 6   **Rose**: "I was raw in every pore."   (Page 11)
        Change lighting to Provence: mid-morning sunshine

Cue 7   **Arthur** bustles out   (Page 12)
        Change lighting to Yorkshire

Cue 8   **Rose**: "…even forgot I had cancer."   (Page 15)
        Change lighting to Provence: hot effect

Cue 9   **Arthur** exits   (Page 16)
        Change lighting to Yorkshire

Cue 10	**Rose**: "Why the fuck did I say that?"	(Page 18)
	Change lighting to Provence	
Cue 11	**Arthur**: "I might get lonely."	(Page 19)
	Slowly fade up Yorkshire lighting: wind and weather effect	
Cue 12	**Rose**: "Just for fun."	(Page 21)
	Change lighting to Provence	
Cue 13	**Rose**: "You do have good ideas, Arthur."	(Page 22)
	Change lighting to Yorkshire	
Cue 14	**Rose**: "…domestic tiffs like ordinary married couples."	(Page 29)
	Change lighting to Provence	

ACT II

To open:	Yorkshire lighting: the middle of the night	
Cue 15	**Rose**: "He might even be right."	(Page 35)
	Change lighting to Provence	
Cue 16	**Arthur**: "One small step for mankind…"	(Page 37)
	Change lighting to Yorkshire: night	
Cue 17	**Rose**: "Just live."	(Page 37)
	Change lighting to late afternoon	
Cue 18	**Rose** sobs	(Page 43)
	The next day	
Cue 19	**Rose**: "Oh, God…"	(Page 52)
	Fade to black	

EFFECTS PLOT

ACT I

Cue 1　　**Arthur** goes out　　　　　　　　　　　　(Page 3)
　　　　　　Sound of car starting and leaving

Cue 2　　Yorkshire lighting up　　　　　　　　　　(Page 10)
　　　　　　Dense smoke billows from the kitchen

Cue 3　　**Ralph** (*off*): "…once we've got this going."　(Page 14)
　　　　　　More smoke billows out

Cue 4　　**Rose**: "I said if it helps to get the work done…"　(Page 14)
　　　　　　Kitchen portable on; twiddle to Radio One

Cue 5　　**Rose** switches on the television　　　　　(Page 28)
　　　　　　TV noise

Cue 6　　**Rose**: "Missed the forecast."　　　　　　(Page 28)
　　　　　　Cut TV noise

ACT II

Cue 7　　**Ralph** stands transfixed, listening　　　(Page 37)
　　　　　　Tape repeats last paragraphs to end

Cue 8　　**Rose**: "…I hope you'll all join in the chorus."　(Page 53)
　　　　　　Sound of car drawing up

Cue 9　　**Rose**: "What else?"　　　　　　　　　(Page 57)
　　　　　　Sound of car drawing up

Cue 10　**Arthur** goes out　　　　　　　　　　　(Page 59)
　　　　　　Sound of car starting up and driving away

PRINTED IN GREAT BRITAIN BY
THE LONGDUNN PRESS LTD., BRISTOL.